Deep Sleep Meditation And Hypnosis

A Step-By-Step Guide To The Most Effective Techniques Help You Get A Good Sleep With Affirmations, Self-Hypnosis, And Mindfulness

Walt Pixar

Table of Contents

Deep Sleep Meditation And Hypnosis

Introduction

This book is here to guide you through everything that you need in order to fall asleep soundly at night. It will teach you all of the mental habits that you need to begin to let go of those daily stressors and anxieties.

It will help you develop the ability and the mindset to release that tension and begin to unwind, and it does through, firstly through instruction on the habits that you need to know, but more importantly, through the use of bedtime stories.

They're not just for children anymore; you, too, can help yourself to fall asleep quickly and soundly through the use of bedtime stories in the form of guided meditation and visualizations. All you have to do is get yourself into bed, get comfortable, relax, and listen.

Part I: Basic Bedtime Stories: Mindfulness and Visualization for Relaxation

C hildren are not the only ones who benefit from reading bedtime stories. In fact, reading before bed for thirty minutes is calmly recommended in nearly any bedtime routine that is meant to help alleviate insomnia.

Bedtime stories work well because they begin to relax you.

You have to be mindful when you read if you want to recall the information, and most of the time, the stories that people choose to read before bed are those that are meant to be enjoyed.

When you read, something special happens. You begin to visualize what you are reading. You can hear the characters interacting in your head. You can see the way they interact, and sometimes, you can even begin to see the images provided for you. This is mindful visualization, and as we have already discussed, that can be one way that you can put the brakes on your anxiety or stress and then begin to focus on the moment. You focus on the words on the page in front of you when you read, or on the words being read to you in the case of an audiobook. You are focused. Your body begins to relax.

Remember, as you read through these, that you can make use of meditations like these on your own as well. After reading through all of these stories, you can choose to explore other environments within your own mind as well. You can choose to focus on the world around you, or go visiting places that you never would have imagined.

As we move on to the mindfulness and visualization meditations, you want to remember to keep yourself somewhere that is comfortable. These are meditations that are designed to help you fall asleep, so they would be best suited to be read or listened to in the comfort of your own bed when you are entirely ready to sleep.

The next time that you are ready to use one of these meditations, begin by taking some time to relax beforehand. Take a shower and unwind. Spend some time quieting your mind. Turn off the screens for at least thirty minutes beforehand and stop for a cup of warm tea. Then, when you are finally ready to sleep, get comfortable in bed and begin using these meditations.

Chapter 1: The Body Light

Take in a big, deep breath, as big as you can make it. Hold it. Five... Four... Three... Two... One... And slowly, exhale it, letting all of the air that you have just released from your body into the world. Then, do it again, taking big, deep breaths that slowly but surely expand your lungs and fill your body with air. With every breath that you take, you will feel calmer. You do not have to do anything at all, just breathe.

Listen to your breath for a moment and focus on it. Hear yourself as you breathe in, and then out again as you continue to get comfortable. Find that perfect spot and be sure that it is the one that you want to be in, as you should try to remain still during the rest of this meditation to ensure that it works well for you. Let go of the tension in your body once more, and you are ready to begin.

Focus inwardly toward the deepest parts of your mind. It could be that your mind exists atop a mountain or amidst a sea of darkness. No matter what the innermost corners of your mind look like, you want to get there, breathing slowly and calmly. Now, imagine that, within your mind, your entire body is lit up. You are gently glowing in the darkness, standing out like a beacon wherever you are. You need to slowly and gently will your body into darkness, and the only way to turn off a body part is to actively tell it to be quiet in the first place. You must go, from head to toe, gently turning off each and every part.

You start out at your toes, on the bottom of your body. You can feel that they are sort of buzzing; that is the energy and tension that they have built up over the course of the day that you must release. That buzzing is there to remind you that you still have to relax that area of your body. It is not unpleasant; it is simply there and tense.

Now, you must move to your ankles, which are glowing brightly after you have released the light from the toes. You flex your right ankle, letting it stretch out as far as it can go and you hold it there as you access it with your mind and shut it off. Then, you release the tension, and your ankle is darker, too. You must now repeat this with your left ankle. You feel the tension in your ankle and you flex your foot as you do so. You hold it tightly for a few moments, and then you release it as quickly as you can, leaving you ankle to remain limp on the bed. Both of your ankles, too, have shut off, along with the feet that they are attached to.

It is time to become aware of you right calf. You can feel that same buzzing of tension within it and, with your next inhale, you tighten up your calf muscle as tightly as you can muster. You hold it, count to three… One… two… three… and release it. It, too, is as relaxed as your feet and the light on it has turned off. Little by little, you work your way throughout your body. Now, you repeat the process with your left calf, tensing it up. Hold your breath… Three… Two… One… And you release it again.

You continue up your body, moving to your right thigh, tensing it up and holding it tightly. As you do, imagine that your body is starting to fill up with relaxation. With the lights out and the energy fading away, you can feel that your toes are beginning to feel very warm and relaxed, and your legs are beginning to sink into the bed. Now, release the thigh and notice how the light turns off within it as well, leaving your right leg entirely turned off. It feels heavy now, and you do not think that you could move it, even if you wanted to.

Now, onto the left thigh, tensing it up. As you do so, imagine that compassion from the universe is flowing in toward you. Imagine that the kindness from the universe, and all of that good, positive energy, is flowing in through your left leg, slowly warming your body and weighing it deeper and deeper into your bed. Now, let go of that tension in your left leg and move on further. It is time for you to move to the next body part.

With your legs entirely off now, it is time to tense and relax your bottom. You will first do your right glute. While you may not be able to see it behind you, it is also glowing brightly. You tense up just your right glute, holding it tense as you turn off the light, and then you let it go. The light fades away and you move on to the left glute, following the same process. You tense it up... You take a deep breath... and you exhale and release the muscle as the light flickers out of existence.

You are beginning to feel incredibly relaxed now; the lower half of your body is almost completely relaxed. You can feel the warmth running through the bottom half with the calmness of the darkness. It is familiar and comfortable, and you want to continue to spread that feeling of relaxation throughout the rest of your body as well.

You move now to your lower back. You can feel that it is buzzing a lot and there is a lot of tension centered there that needs to be released as soon as you can.

You move now to your abs; they are also glowing incredibly brightly, showing that they are, in fact, holding far more tension than you may have realized. It may take you a little bit longer to alleviate the tension here. Take a big breath in, feeling it swell within your belly and then tense down the abdominal muscles for a moment. Three... Two... One... and release. As you exhale, let out the tension in your abs and move down the line.

You move up to your shoulder blades, which hold a high level of tension as well. With your focus on your shoulders, you feel them buzzing. You feel that tension that will prevent you from sleeping. Tighten the muscles in your shoulders, gathering up the buzzing within them and release it, suddenly removing all tension from the area.

You feel like most of your body now is melting away, deeper and deeper into the bed underneath you. Revel in the feeling of relaxation that is filling you and think about how you can achieve bringing that same degree of relaxation elsewhere into your body as well. Take a big deep breath once more, and pay attention to how your lower body feels, and remember that feeling. You want that everywhere.

Next, it is time to move upward. Your shoulders are still glowing and they are still quite tense. It is time to focus on them, tightening up the muscles there so you can release it all with just a deep breath. Hold on to that tension for a few moments, tightening up the muscles, and then let it go. Now, all that remains that has not been touched are your neck and your head.

Your neck can hold a lot of tension throughout the day and you may see that it is glowing very brightly within you. Feel the back of your neck and tense up the muscles there as well. You must work to gather up each and every last sensation of buzzing within it and release it, and you do so.

Now, it is time to move up to the head. Start with your jaw. Feel it now as it is, and then clench it as tightly as you can without hurting your teeth, holding it for a few moments, and then releasing all of the tension. Then, repeat it with your cheek muscles—pull your lips into the widest smile that you can, holding it there, and then let it go. Furrow your brows together, as if you are angry, and then release that, as well. Little by little, release all of that tension that you had in your face, until your entire body is completely and utterly at ease.

Now, with your eyes still closed, sit and feel your body, completely free of tension. Feel the gentle calmness that flows within you. Feel as the sensation of heaviness, the relaxation that you have been working to instill throughout your body, flows up. It starts at your feet, which, when standing will be the base to your entire stance; they are like your roots, sucking up the comfort and the relaxation from the earth and slowly bringing it up throughout your body.

Pay attention as the rest of your body feels so warm and well-rested. Enjoy the sensation of relaxation as you remain in this position and really revel in it. Love the warmth and let it embrace your body, gentle and soft like a cloud cradling it.

Now, continue your deep breathing. Breathe in… and out… And in… and out…

You are sinking deeper, now… You are calmer than you have ever been before right now… You are relaxed and you are heavy right now… And you are ready to sleep…

Every breath brings you closer and closer to sleep. Every breath brings you closer and closer to that utter relaxation, that gentle embrace of true sleep that you are searching to get. Keep up your deep breathing until you finally, gently, drift off to sleep…

Chapter 2: The Sleep Blossoms

L et's begin by taking in some big, deep breaths. These breaths should be gentle and natural… Follow your own natural rhythm as you breathe in, and then out, over and over again. Just be present in your body and breathe for a few moments to yourself. In… And out… In… And out… With every breath that you take, imagine that you are getting lighter, and yet, as you continue to get lighter, you somehow manage to sink deeper and deeper into your bed.

Enjoy the moment…

Take a breath in, and hold it this time. Five… Four… Three… Two… One… And let it go, slowly and gently, through your lips. Imagine that you are gently blowing on a candle, not so strongly that the candle will go out, but just enough so the flame dances about. Take in another breath, right through your nose, and hold it. Five… Four… Three… Two… One… And exhale again, just as gently and just as slowly as before. Now, one more breath. In… Five… Four… Three… Two… One… And out…

Now, as you feel yourself sinking deeply into your bed, deeper and deeper as you begin to relax, close your eyes if they are not already closed. Imagine for a moment that you are sitting right underneath a beautiful tree. The tree is a cherry tree, and it is in bloom. The cherry tree is right next to a quiet stream that is passing by, and you move, in your mind, toward the tree. You can smell the soft, gently sweet scent of the delicate cherry blossoms, and you sit right underneath it. Your back, in your mind, rests against the tree's strong trunk, and you feel supported. You know that this tree will hold your weight and it will keep you there for as long as you would like to be.

As you sit underneath this cherry tree, you watch the stream. It is not a very big stream, nor is it deep, but it flows by gently. Imagine its sound as it flows past you, gently babbling away. You sit there and listen to the babbling of the stream and you breathe in and out, enjoying the relaxing, calming scent of the blossoms and sinking deeper into relaxation.

Feel your body sink deeper into your bed, and imagine that the relaxation is moving everywhere throughout your body, leaving it feeling as warm as you like. Feel the bed providing you with the support, gently conforming to your body, but still holding you up where you need to be, keeping your back nice and straight, just like you need. Feel that same support that you felt from the tree reminding you that you are sturdy and safe and strong.

Then, move back into your mind, retreating back to that image of you underneath the cherry tree. You sit there, tall and supported and relaxed, and then a breeze passes by. It is not a strong breeze at all; the leaves on the tree and the blades of grass underneath you barely quiver as it washes over them, and yet suddenly, you see a cloud of pink pass you by. But, upon closer inspection, it is not a cloud at all; it is a wave of pink cherry blossoms that have been moved from the tree! The blossoms slowly drift downward, falling into the water all around you, and then you notice something; the stream is not very powerful, either. The blossoms drift onto the surface of the stream and slowly and lazily drift away, spinning in slow circles as they are moved.

Watch each petal as they drift away. Pay attention to each one for a moment or two as you work through this. The first petal that you see, lazily drifting through the water's slow currents, is the anxiety surrounding your day. You must watch that anxiety, waiting for it to flow down the stream. You might feel the urge to pick it up or to hold onto it or to try to force it down into the water to drown it, but that will not work. The only way to be rid of it is to let it pass you by as slowly and as gently as possible. The only way that you can really help it along is by letting it go and by breathing.

You take in a great, big inhale, breathing in that soft scent once more. Hold it... Five... Four... Three... Two... One... And exhale it. Let that air out, and watch as your anxiety goes around a bend in the stream, out of sight and out of mind. The water in front of you is clear... and then you see more petals coming your way as well. Just like before, the only way that you can help these petals to pass is to help them to go on their own without any resistance on your part. You must simply watch as they slowly and quietly drift away.

The next petal that drifts in front of you is the petal that holds your fear. Remember, your fears are a little bit different from your anxiety; your anxiety is there before the fear. The fears are the thoughts that you have that scare you, and they must also be released into the stream to keep on flowing and to stay away.

You breathe again, deeper this time if you can. In… And hold it… Five… Four… Three… Two… One… And exhale. You notice that, with that exhale, the petal gets a little bit further away from you. It drifts a little bit further down the stream. You take another big, deep, diaphragmatic breath, breathing in… And holding it… And out… And again… And again…

And after you have breathed in and out long enough, the petal of fear, too, drifts away. It disappears around the bend, leaving your mind a little bit freer for a little bit longer.

Now, another petal drifts in front of you—three, actually, and you realize that they are sort of stuck together by something sticky, perhaps sap or nectar or something. These petals are your tension, your stress, and your worry. They are a bit heavier than the other petals, and they go a bit slower as they go past you. They get stuck on a small plant in front of you, simply sitting there without anywhere to go, and as the petals are stuck, you, too, are weighed down by your stress, your tension, and your worry. You need to release them, too, and the only way to release them is through breathing deeply and slowly to fill your body with relaxation to force those feelings out and allow you to feel other feelings instead.

You breathe in… and out… In… and out…

Soon, as you return back to your cherry tree, you see that the petals have become dislodged, and they are floating away from you. You can see them disappear out of sight, and therefore out of your mind for the night.

You realize that, as you sit against the tree, you feel quite relaxed. You are enjoying your current feelings, and you feel like your heart is floating just as daintily and gracefully as the blossoms as they fell… But then, you realize that there are many more pink spots within the stream that is your mind. They are spots that will have to be cleared out, too.

You breathe in… And the blossom drifts in front of you. This one brings with it the feeling of peace that you feel in being chosen by a young puppy or kitten that wants to cuddle with you to sleep. It is that peace of heart and that love that you feel when the baby animal curls up in your lap, entirely of its own volition. It is that feeling of being sought out and chosen to bring comfort to someone else, unprompted. It is warm... It is pleasant... It is relaxing... And the blossom drifts away.

You take another breath. This time, the blossom brings with it the sense of fulfilment when someone tells you that you have done a great job. It is that sense of pride for yourself, of being able to do something wondrous and getting it right. It is that fulfillment that comes, perhaps after spending a long time trying to get the work right, or having done so on the first time after you had worked so very hard to prepare. You bask in the sensation... And the blossom drifts away.

You are beginning to feel very sleepy now.

You breathe in again... And another beautiful pink blossom drifts in front of you. It lingers there, hanging on the water as it spins gently in the current, like a child gently twirling an umbrella to watch the colors change. And with this blossom, you feel the gentle admiration of nature itself; the quiet appreciation that you feel for the world around you and how everything is interconnected. You feel at ease in the moment; you feel like you are entirely calm in that second, and then, the blossom drifts away.

You do not have to stay awake... Do not fight the sensation of sleepiness as it gently leads you into its soft, soothing embrace.

You take another deep breath in... And as you do, you watch the next blossom float in front of you, this one carrying with it the gentle feeling of comfort that you have not felt since you were a child; that comfort that you feel when you embrace your parents and feel their pure, unconditional love for you as they hold you close and keep you safe. You feel entirely cradled in their embrace, free from harm, and you bask in it. Let the feeling continue to carry you deeper and deeper into your relaxation.

It will not be long now… You are getting so sleepy that you could not open your eyes, even if you wanted to. You are entirely nestled into your bed, warm, safe, happy, relaxed, and calm… You are comfortable… You are safe… You are happy… You are loved… And you are ready to sleep.

Chapter 3: The Magic Words

C lose your eyes and take a deep, cleansing breath. Hold your inhale in your lungs, feeling as they expand gently, and then let it all out. Breathe in again, holding on to the feeling of expansion and feel your very mind expanding as well. With every breath that you take, feel the barriers of your mind continue to open up, more and more, little by little, until you feel more relaxed than ever. You are not thinking about anything at all right now, and the only things in your attention are your deep breaths and these words...

You must scan your body for tension now, so you can let it all go. Let's start with your head... If you feel anything, release it. Take in a deep breath... And exhale... And move on to your face. Release the tension that you feel in your face. Inhale... Exhale... And down to your jaw. Feel it in that moment; is it tense? Release the tension. Inhale... Exhale... Release. And move down to the neck. Inhale... Exhale... Release. And down to the shoulders and shoulder blades. Inhale... Exhale... Release. And down to the chest muscles. Inhale... Exhale... Release. Down to your abs. Inhale... Exhale... Release. And your lower back. Inhale... Exhale... Release. Move to your glutes. Inhale... Exhale...

Release. And your thighs. Inhale… Exhale… Release. You are almost done now. Move down to your calves. Inhale… Exhale… Release. And your ankles. Inhale… Exhale… Release. And finally, your toes. Inhale… Exhale… Release.

By now, your entire body likely feels very, very calm. You have allowed yourself to let go of all of that tension that has built up over the course of a day weighing you down, holding you back, and keeping you from your sleep… And with the weight of the day lifted, you can begin to relax. It is time for you to quietly and calmly begin deep breathing once more. We are going to go through deep breathing exercises along with affirmations.

These affirmations are magical. They work when you believe them—when you *really* believe them. Your affirmations are your intentions. They are there to help you fix both your body and your mind, connecting them together and soothing you into a quiet, restful, restorative sleep that your body needs. In between each deep breath, you will hear a soft, gentle, sleep-related affirmation. Focus on the affirmations, and feel them—really feel them within yourself. Listen to the magic words. Let them work their magic. Let yourself be relaxed, guided gently to sleep by these words as they fill your mind.

Breathe in and hold it. Five… Four… Three… Two… One… And exhale slowly. Five… Four… Three… Two… One.

You are beginning to feel relaxed and at ease. You feel your body beginning to sink into the bed. Now, repeat these magic words to yourself, and really feel them within your body and mind. Know that these words are true as you repeat them. Really accept and embrace these words so the magic can work.

"Today, I have done everything that I possibly could, and I tried my hardest. I cannot do anything right now to change what has happened earlier and I should not focus on this right now."

Breathe in and hold it. Five... Four... Three... Two... One... And exhale slowly. Five... Four... Three... Two... One.

Your mind is feeling relaxed and at ease... You feel calmer now and you feel your anxieties drifting away, one by one, and passing you by. Repeat these magic words to yourself:

"My bed is a place of sleep, away from the anxiety. I am away from the fear and the anger. I am away from the stress. My bed is a place of calmness and relaxation, and no stress can get me here. I release my stress and banish it from the comfort of my bed."

Breathe in and hold it. Five... Four... Three... Two... One... And exhale slowly. Five... Four... Three... Two... One.

Now, you can feel some of your fear begin to fade away as well. The fear of failure or the feel of being insufficient is fading away. You can see those insecurities disappearing, fading away from your bed. You repeat these magic words to yourself as you feel your body sink deeper into your bed:

"It is time for me to relax and heal. Sleep is healing and restorative and I will sleep soundly and calmly tonight in the safety and comfort of my own bed. Right now, in this moment, I do not have to do anything but relax and allow my body to heal itself. It will heal when it is time and I will be able to fall asleep with ease when I am ready."

Breathe in and hold it. Five... Four... Three... Two... One... And exhale slowly. Five... Four... Three... Two... One.

"I will fall asleep and I will stay asleep. It will be okay if I wake up tonight, because if I do, my body will know what to do to help ensure that I get all of the sleep that I will need tonight. It will not let me go without the rest that I need."

Breathe in and hold it. Five... Four... Three... Two... One... And exhale slowly. Five... Four... Three... Two... One.

You can feel that sleep coming in closer and closer, and although it is not quite there yet, you know that it will be soon; you can feel it lingering just out of reach, brushing against your mind like a feather rubbed just above your skin. You can feel it there, beginning to dull your senses. You can feel your mind starting to slow and you can feel your body giving in to the sleep. You tell yourself some more magic words:

"I am perfectly relaxed right this moment, and I am content with that. I accept myself in this moment and I know that, when I need to, I can do what I must to do the right thing at the right time. I do not need to worry about anything but getting the rest that I will need to ensure that I do the right thing."

Breathe in and hold it. Five… Four… Three… Two… One… And exhale slowly. Five… Four… Three… Two… One.

As you take this breath, you are almost there; you are right on the brink of sleep and you can feel yourself teetering over the edge. You are ready to give in; you are ready to let go and to welcome that comfort that will come with the sleep that you know that your body needs. As you begin to fall asleep, you tell yourself one last thing. You repeat one more set of magic affirmations to carry you off to sleep:

"I am exactly where I need to be, both in the moment and in life. I accept myself, both in this moment and in my life. I love myself, both in this moment and in my life. I embrace this moment. I embrace myself."

And now, you gently and calmly drift off to sleep. If you wake up again, you know that you will be okay, and you trust that your body will be able to take care of you perfectly in the moment.

Chapter 4: Gratitude

Take in a great, big, deep breath. Feel it as it floods within your lungs, blowing them up, and stretching them out, and then release the tension within them, exhaling calmly and quietly into the world around you. Breathe in again… Feel that relaxation within you as you breathe deeply… And exhale it. And once more, breathe in… And out…

Get comfortable in your bed. Find exactly the right spot that is perfect for you. It will be perfectly comfortable for you, no matter what the position is. Perhaps you like to rest with your head curled inward, knees up against your chest, or you rest like a starfish in the center of the bed. No matter where that position is for you, get to it, and relax.

Take in a breath, and as you do, feel all of your tensions and frustrations from the day filling your breath. Let your lungs fill with air and let the air that you breathe in take away the tensions in your body. Your lungs, with your heart, give you life. They bring you the breath that you need to keep yourself alive. As your lungs do their job, filling up with oxygen to exchange with carbon dioxide from within your body, thank your lungs for being the filters that keep your body clean. Thank your lungs for removing the waste and allowing you to continue to breath. Feel grateful that you have working lungs that will allow you to take that deep breath and hold it.

Breathe in and hold it. As you hold it, direct all of the love and gratitude to your lungs. Five… Four… Three… Two… One… And exhale. Repeat this once more, sending your lungs that same quiet gratitude for everything that they do to keep you alive. In… And out…

Now, focus on your heart within your chest. You may be able to feel it as soon as you turn your focus to it, or you may need to rest a hand atop your heart to feel your pulse. Feel the beating of your heart, that great muscle that expands and contracts, over and over again, tirelessly bringing to your body the blood that you need, filled with the oxygen given to you by your kind lungs. Focus on this for a moment and let yourself feel the love for your heart. *Thump-thump. Thump-thump. Thump-thump.* With every contraction of your heart, remind yourself that your heart is working endlessly. While you sleep, your heart will be there, working hard to keep you alive. It will send all of the blood that your body will need to all of the right places and it will work as much as it can to help you.

Focus on your feet now. Breathe in deeply and hold it... Five... Four... Three... Two... one... And thank your feet for everything that they do. Even when you are at your weakest, your feet are there for you. They support you, even when you feel like you cannot support yourself. Even when the stress and the anxiety is overwhelming, your feet are there. They are there to hold you up, even when you feel weak, and they will do this without you even having to think about it.

Send your feet that same gratitude. Thank them for keeping you standing up on your own, even when you felt like you were not.

They were there for you endlessly and thanklessly, holding up and supporting your weight, and that is a job that is worthy of thanks.

Breathe in... And out... And send another feeling of thanks to your feet before moving on.

Your spine has been there for you. It has been the support that your body needed; while the feet held you up, your back kept your head up. It supported you. It provided you with that stable base to be able to stand in the first place. It gave the feet what they needed to keep you up, and that is a worthy job indeed. Without your back, you would not be able to stand up. You would not be able to move. You would not be able to hold your head up high, or at all. Your spine's support has allowed you to do everything that you have ever done, and it does so without you really being aware of it.

Send your spine that gratitude that you have shared for the rest of your body now. Give your spine that feeling of gratefulness that you need to best cope with the world around you. Remind yourself that, at the end of the day, you can stand because you have your spine's support.

Breathe in, and hold it... Five... Four... Three... two... One... And exhale.

And now, focus on your whole body. Become fully aware of each and every part of you, from your head to your toes and everything in between. As you become aware of your entire body, it is time for you to send gratitude to it all. Quietly and gently focus on your entire body for a while, respecting it and everything that it has done for you. Remind yourself that your body is there to help you tirelessly. Remind yourself that your body works for you, even when you do not want to move. Remind yourself that your body is perfectly capable of providing you what you need, and it will provide you with that sleep that you need exactly when you are ready to sleep. Focus on your body for a moment and feel how it feels right in this moment. Does it feel sleepy? Stressed? Tense? You can help your body to become right. Does your body feel exhausted? Let yourself sit in quiet relaxation. But, more importantly, before you do that, create a very special thank you for your body.

Focus on your entire body and feel the clam and gentle love that you have to give for it. Take all of that respect and admiration that you have given to each part of yourself and return it to your body as well. Provide your body with exactly what it needs—that admiration from you. That appreciation. That acknowledgement that, at the end of the day, your body is working for you.

Take in a big, deep breath. In… Hold… And out… Thank your body again. Then, breathe in… And out… And again. And breathe in… And out…

Now, turn your attention quietly to your mind. Take a good, long look at your mind within yourself. It may be anxious. It may be afraid. It may be feeling anything at all. No matter what it is feeling, stop and say a quiet, gentle thank you to your mind. Remind yourself that your mind is exactly what you need it to be. Remind yourself that your mind is perfectly imperfect. It is perfectly you, and that is exactly what it is supposed to be.

Give it one last thank you as you take in another deep breath. Let yourself fill up with gratitude for your body and your mind. Let yourself focus on the ways in which you love yourself, and there are ways that you are valuable. There are ways that you are worthy of love. You are perfectly you and that is enough.

Now, with that final thank you to your mind, it is time to sleep…

Close your eyes. Empty your mind. Leave behind the feelings of gratitude within yourself and let yourself drift within yourself. Let your mind begin to wander and let sleep wash over you. It may start slowly at first, gently lapping at your toes, and slowly building up until your entire body is tired. Wait for the feelings of sleepiness as they fill your body. Welcome them as they do. Thank them as they do, and allow yourself to relax completely.

Do not fight the waves of sleep as they come over you. Do not fight your body. Do not fight your mind. Simply allow yourself to quietly drift off to sleep once and for all within the comfort of your own bed.

Chapter 5: The Anxiety Star

Close your eyes and take a deep breath. Feel the breath as it fills up your body. Bask in the sensations of feeling your body stretch and relax. Stretch out as much as you feel the need to do, working the energy within yourself and allowing all of your muscles to shift to exactly where they need to go. You can feel your muscles within yourself, each of them tense and filled with stress and anxiety.

Take a deep breath. Remember, you are strong. You are capable. You are dependable. You can do this. All you have to do is believe in yourself and it will come. Take a dep breath and hold it. Count to five slowly. One… Two… Three… Four… Five… And exhale it. Let all of the air that you were holding in your lungs escape. Focus on your breathing and how it feels within you. Pay attention to the ways that you can control your breath. Pay attention to the methods that you use as you breathe and the way that you feel as you do. Notice how your stomach moves, welcoming the breath as it fills you up. Notice how it feels when you let it go afterward. Pay attention to that shifting in breathing as it happens, and remember that, at the end of the day, your breathing is a powerful thing.

Your breath brings you life-giving oxygen.

Your breath lets go of the waste that your body creates.

Your breath can calm you down when you are scared.

It can wake you up when you are feeling tired, or it can help you settle down to sleep.

Your breath is perhaps one of the most powerful tools that you have, and you can use it. You can make sure that you feel relaxed. You can make sure that you feel brave and strong. You can make sure that you feel ready to sleep, and all you need is your breath.

Take in a deep breath and hold it... Five... Four... Three... Two... One... And exhale it. Feel the air—really feel it—as you blow it out. Notice the way that it passes your tongue, cooling the damp surface as it passes. Feel how it caresses your lips as you round them into a small, but loose, O shape. Imagine blowing out a candle; that is the shape that you want your lips to take.

Take in a breath again… And with this breath, feel your body filling with warmth. Feel the gentle air filing up your lungs, and imagine this wonderful warmth emanating from your lungs. You are breathing in love. You are breathing in life. You are breathing in the very essence of this wondrous and mysterious world that we do not yet entirely understand. You are breathing in the remnants of what was once star dust, drifting aimlessly throughout the vast vacuum of space, that endless expanse of nothingness—and now it is within your lungs.

Breathe in again, once again marveling in the wonders that are life within yourself. Hold the breath, and exhale. In that exhale, imagine that all of your fears are fading away.

You are invaluable.

Breathe in again, and as you do, remember, those lungs are rare. That body is a rarity. Your existence is a rarity that deserves to be lived. You deserve to be proud that you exist; you should be proud to live on a planet with odds that were so incredibly stacked up against it, and yet it made life happen. That alone is something that is worthy of celebration.

Recognize that inner value within yourself, and that inner strength that you hold. Breathe out the fears, the anxiety, the insecurities, and the stress. Remember, a star bows to no one. A star blinks on, endlessly in the night. The star will flicker on, burning brightly in the sky, no matter who is watching, and no matter what is paying attention. The star deserves to do this because it is so vast, so great, and so mystical.

You, too, are the ancestor of a star. You have the ancestral bloodline of those stars that shine so incredibly brightly above you and that alone is worthy of celebration.

So, with your powerful, beautiful star lungs, take in a deep breath and hold it.

Now, imagine your anxieties within you. Gather them up, one by one. Pick up all of those thoughts that bring with them fear, anxiety, stress, or anything else that is negative. Build up those feelings within yourself with your next deep breath. As you breathe in, you bring all of those anxieties to the star. You give them to the star, and the star within you burns them. The star within you lights them up and begins to transform them. The star releases them out into the world. It takes your stress. It takes your anxiety. It takes them all and then it burns them as fuel, making you shine brighter than ever before. Each and every one of your anxieties get thrown into the star, one by one, and as they burn within you, you begin to feel calmer. You begin to feel settled down. You begin to recognize that you will be okay after all. You remember that, at the end of the day, you are valuable.

As the star burns away the last of your anxiety, you are left feeling calmer. You feel relaxed. You have breathed out the last of your anxieties for the night, and that leaves you feeling better than ever. You are calm... You feel your body beginning to relax, now that all of that negativity is gone.

You feel relaxed as you breathe...

You breathe in deeply, in... and out... You feel the energy within yourself burning brightly as you continue to breathe. But soon, that energy begins to quiet down. That energy becomes calmer. That energy becomes a warm, gentle blanket that can envelope you. It keeps you comforted and leaves you feeling warm, deep within yourself. It leaves you feeling restful, deep within yourself. It leaves you feeling capable of living through anything as you focus inwardly.

Now, it is just you and the star... Shining warmly and comfortingly, within yourself... You feel yourself beginning to relax from head to toe. Without the stressors of the anxiety weighing you down, you feel almost weightless; as if you could defy gravity and begin to float right then and there.

Breathe in and hold it... Five... The star is beginning to slow down. Four... The star's light begins to dull. Three... the star begins to grow smaller and smaller within you. Two... the star is duller now and you can barely see the light. One... it fades away. But, the star is not gone forever; it is simply taking a nap within you, leaving you with a warm, barely pulsating light that gently glows to the beat of your own heart. It is there within you for whenever you need it. It is there to give you that added boost whenever you need it, to guide you to sleep when you feel like you need the most help and it is there to do that for you.

As the star fades away, you feel all of its energy fade, too. Instead, you are left with a quiet sleepiness and a familiar warmth within your heart. You feel the quiet glow of the star within you and know that you have no reason to be anxious any longer, for all you have to do to call back the star is to breathe deeply and intend for the anxiety to melt away. If you can remember to do that, you know that you can defeat any anxiety that comes your way.

Now, you let yourself begin to relax, letting your body melt into the bed. You can feel yourself fading now, just like the star did... You can feel yourself growing sleepier and sleepier. You feel your very mind beginning to ebb and flow, just like the star's light, and you reach out in your mind. You reach out for that comforting warmth that your star has brought to you. With that warmth embraced within your mind, you can feel it spreading throughout your entire body, from place to place. You can feel that warmth allowing you to thrive. You can feel that warmth gently carrying your mind with it to that same quiet, dark place that your star retreated to.

Your mind feels fuzzy now; do not fight the warm, inviting embrace of sleep. Let the embrace take you. Let it engulf you completely and gently lull you into that warm, comfortable place in the depths of your mind. Let it lead you back to that place, where your star is waiting for you. The warmth leads you, and you can see it there, faintly at first, but as you get closer and closer to sleep, you see the star growing brighter and brighter.

Breathe in and hold it. Five... Four... Three... Two... One... And let it go.

And with that breath, you let your mind fade off to sleep.

Chapter 6: The Breath of Relaxation and the Sea of Sleep

Your day is done; it is time for you to begin to relax, to unwind, and to release all of the tension within your body. It is a time of great potential; you have the potential to be able to get the sleep and rest that you will need to give you energy for the next day. You have the potential to go on fantastical dreams to far off places that you have never heard of before. You have the potential to get that comfort that you will need to ensure that you enjoy your last, quiet moments of consciousness before your body fades off to sleep.

Take in a deep breath in your bed. Settle down as the air fills your lungs, and feel your body sinking deeper into your mattress. Hold the air in your lungs for a moment, and let yourself enjoy the breath. And then, let it slip away. Imagine that your breath is a gentle breeze, and it carries away any of your reservations about your day. It takes with it the anxiety about the day that you have led. It takes away the stress that you have felt, leaving behind space for the good feelings of the day. It removes your stressors and your frustrations. It removes your tensions and your fears. It leaves you feeling cleansed, relaxed, and able to take on the world with ease.

Take in another deep breath and hold it for five seconds. Five... Four... Three... Two... One... And let it go again. Again, imagine that your breath is removing more of that negativity from your life. It is removing all of the stress, all of the tension, and anything else that would hold you back, and you are allowing it to do so.

You breathe again, and soon, you notice that your shoulders are sinking in deeper into your bed. Your bed is beginning to feel very warm with all of the breaths that you are taking. It is beginning to feel very tired, very relaxed, and very ready to sleep every time that you take in and let go of a breath.

Sit back and quietly feel the way that your body feels. Do not fight off any of your tensions. Do not do anything at all; today, you are a quiet observer to the feelings that you have throughout your body. Today, you are simply watching as the world passes you by. You are watching yourself as your body shifts underneath the waves of sleepiness that are coming your way.

You take in another breath, and with this one, you can feel sleepiness washing over you. It starts at your feet and moves up your body in waves, emanating from your toes, flowing up your legs, past the knees, over the thighs, and into your chest. You can feel the sleepiness just as heavily as your blanket that is above you.

Get comfortable now; find that spot that you like to sleep in. You know the one—it is the one that you go to every time it is time to unwind and every time that it is time to sleep. This is the most comfortable spot for you and you alone; it can be any position, so long as it brings you comfort. It brings you joy and it brings you that feeling of safety.

As you settle into that spot, let yourself nestle down into it, getting the spot just right for you. Feel the warmth that begins to fill your body and stop and pay attention. Do you feel any tension throughout your body right now? Where is it?

Starting at your head and working down to your toes, check in with each and every body part, releasing the tensions that you hold and freeing yourself from the negativity that would otherwise overwhelm you. Allow yourself to relax entirely. Allow that tension and that negativity to free itself on its own, without your intervention.

As your body begins to shift around, you feel another wave of sleep. This one is heavier than the last one, but it is not overwhelming. You can feel it as it creeps its way up your body, little by little, leaving behind the telltale signs of tiredness. As it washes over you, you take in a deep inhale. The breath seems to give it more strength; it begins to feel even more comforting as you hold... And then exhale...

Notice what your body is doing and relax. If you find tension within your body, try to let it go now. Now, it is time to work out those feelings of tension. Now, it is time to figure out how to loosen up your body and your mind. Now, you can work hard to let yourself feel comfortable in your position. Now, you can unwind and relax.

Take in another breath, and this time, as you do, imagine that your mind is filled with clouds. Imagine that each and every cloud is a thought in your mind. They can be worries, or thoughts, or simply random facts; no matter the thought, they must all be blown away. Imagine that your breath, deep, strong, nurturing, and life-giving, gets to blow away all of these thoughts that are there to distract you. Imagine that breath form your lungs blowing across the skies, gently but powerfully. Imagine that breath gently coaxing those clouds away from you and giving you the quiet time that you will need to allow yourself to rest. Allow yourself to relax deeper and deeper into the bed.

As the last cloud fades away, long gone, you can take another deep breath. This time, hold it and let the warmth from your breath fill the body. Your breath is powerful; your breath can help you to unwind. It can help to melt the stress in your body like butter, pushing it away and clearing your thoughts. It can work hard to ensure that, at the end of the day, you are able to sleep.

Feel any lingering tension begin to melt as you exhale that time and focus on the feelings of sleepiness that were left behind. Focus on that feeling of heaviness. The heaviness starts in your feet, where the next wave of sleep washes over you. This one feels heavy and overwhelming, but pleasantly so. It is like the overwhelming urge to give a puppy a pet, or to give a hug to a loved one; you want to embrace the heaviness of the sleep, to welcome it, and to follow it.

Let the wave of sleep begin to guide you. Let the wave wash over you and then pick you up. Let the wave carry your mind away with it. Let the wave carry your mind to sleep. Do not resist it at all as it comes to you; let it carry you. Help it carry you.

The first wave does not bring you there, but you feel heavy. Your eyes are too heavy to open now and you feel the weight of the entire world all around you as your body grows sleepier than ever. The next wave comes with the next breath and as it does, you feel even sleepier than before. You feel like the edges of your mind are beginning to grow fuzzy. You gently scan your body once more, and every single muscle within your body is ready to sleep. Every single muscle within your body has let go of their tensions. Every single muscle is ready to embrace the wave, to ride with it, and to let it take total control of your body and your mind. Every single muscle has given up resistance.

Breathe in deeply through your nose. You are almost there... It will not be long now... You feel relaxed... You feel sleepy... You feel your mind fading as it gives in to the sleep that you are so close to... Breathe out...

You are so sleepy now that you cannot move at all. Not a single muscle in your body is working. Breathe in... You are right there on the edge as another wave of sleepiness comes your way. It rides up your body, covering you like a warm blanket, embracing you the way a mother embraces her child. It rocks you gently and calmly. Breathe out...

You are so close to sleep now. The wave of sleep takes you away, carrying you out to the sea of sleep. You let it gently pull you away. Breathe in... Five... Four... Three... two... one... And breathe out...

You continue gently breathing as the sea of sleep gently rocks you to sleep.

Part II: Stress Patterns and How to Understand Them

The first thing that you must learn to do when you are trying to defeat your stress is to learn how you can identify it. You must be able to stop and check in with your body to determine whether or not you *are* stressed. You need to have the wherewithal to stop yourself in the moment to check in with yourself. You need to be self-aware enough to realize that the tension that is filling your body right that moment, making you feel like you are ready to jump out of your own skin in the moment, is thanks to the stress that you are enduring.

Stress, once you learn to recognize it, is readily apparent in the body. It can be found relatively simply just through doing what is known as a body scan, in which you will slowly and steadily go throughout your body, one area at a time, in order to try to identify how you are feeling.

Widespread tension throughout the body is just one of the places in which you can identify that you are feeling stress.

Along with tension, your body begins to wear on itself. You start to ache more   often, all over your body. You may constantly feel achy, but not know why or where the aches started. You may feel like you are miserable in other ways as well—it could be, for example, that you begin to feel physically drained.

You feel like your muscles are sore, or like you have run a marathon, even if you have done nothing but sleep. You may feel like you suffer from headaches more often than ever. This is because stress causes problems for the body. The body has a natural stress response—it is meant to have its own way to tolerate the pressures of life so it can survive. However, long-term, that stress weighs on the body.

Think of it like sprinting—you may be able to sprint and push that quick burst of energy for a short period of time, but you cannot sustain that sprint, no matter how hard you try to do so. At some point, likely sooner rather than later, you will have to slow down.

The sprint will weigh on you and it will wear you out. Stress, too will weigh at you until you can no longer continue to maintain it. When you get to that point of chronic stress, where you are constantly fighting against feeling of distress, you get to a point in which your body does get impacted.

Your body is preparing for a battle. Your body is preparing to the best of its ability to fight off a threat—a perceived danger of some sort that it believes will be a problem. Your body thinks that what is happening is dangerous in some sense. It does not discriminate between whether that threat is to your physical or mental wellbeing—rather, it responds with avoidance and an attempt to defend itself nonetheless.

In fight or flight mode, what happens is that your body becomes stressed. Your body becomes flooded with all sorts of hormones that are meant to keep you motivated and keep you safe. However, they also wear down your body. Insomnia becomes common.

Your body elevates the heart and blood pressure as well, which can also be a major risk factor for you. Your body will be flooded with glucose in an attempt to give you the energy that you need to run or fight, but over a long period of time, this can lead to you becoming diabetic later down the line.

Chapter 7: How Stress Develops: From Birth to Adulthood

Even before birth, babies can endure stress. Pregnant women, especially toward the end of pregnancy, go through what is known as fetal non-stress tests.

It is oftentimes stress caused by a lack of oxygen or other problems with the placenta that can be harmful to the body. Babies, in a particularly stressful birth, may release meconium during birth or into the amniotic fluid in the womb, potentially due to stress.

As children age, they are inundated with stress as well—they can be exposed to stress from parents or from school. They can find that they live in a stressful environment or find that they are worried about having their needs met at any point in time.

However, the older the child, typically the more stressed they become as well. Stress can be a major problem for children and can have adverse effects on their development as well.

As children move into the teenage and adult years, stressors continue to compound. Generally speaking, the more responsibilities that someone has, the more likely that it becomes that stress will ramp up at some point or another.

Childhood Stress

Stress for children seems like a bit of an impossibility for many parents. They think that their children could not actually be that stressed out; after all, all they have to do is wake up, eat, play, go to school, and sleep, right? What is so bad about that?

However, just because you do not think that it is stressful does not mean that it is actually not stressful for the children. Children do not yet have that life experience that drains on them. They do not yet have those responsibilities of adults, but to them, their stress is legitimate and is real. They feel that strain on themselves just as much as an adult, and sometimes, even more because of the fact that they are unable to really understand what is going on. They are unable to articulate themselves in ways that would help them to eliminate some of that stress before it can be allowed to fester. Instead, they sit in their stress without any real way to fix them.

A lot of the stress in children's lives either comes form the too-packed schedules that we push on them these days; children are told that they have to go to school, study, play sports, do their chores, and so much more, all without ever getting that time that hey really need to allow them to better cope with the world around them.

They can feel stress because they are too busy and do not get the time that they need to unwind. They can become stressed by their life and the environment that they live in; it could be that they are suffering from being stuck at home with parents that argue too much. It could be that the news on television has been distressing, or someone in the home is sick. It could be a problem with the environment itself.

Stress in children also does not usually present in the same way that it does with adults. Adults can, at the very least, talk out the problems and begin to work on solving them. Children, however, are usually stuck. They are quite powerless, all things considered. They do not have the capability to go off on their own.

They typically, especially preteen, cannot go off on their own yet. They are not allowed to distance themselves out from the stressors that they face, so they cannot address stress the way many adults do. However, the stress in children can be identifiable if you know what to look for. It could be biting nails or sucking thumbs. It could be acting out or bullying other children in an attempt to control what they can. It could also show up as sudden changes, typically negative, in academic performance.

Teenage Stress

Like children, teens are also susceptible to stress, and oftentimes, they find that they are actually even more susceptible than the younger children.

Stress is related to the demands on children and the more that children get older and develop, the more pressures that are dumped onto them. By the teenage years, children are oftentimes juggling between six and nine classes for school.

They probably have their sports that they are in. They want to fit in and make sure that they get along with their peers. They want to be liked. They feel the mounting pressure of college and adulthood, looming just around the horizon.

For teens, stress is typically piled on by school—stress is something that is reported by the vast majority of students. They may report that they are stressed out about the testing or about making sure that they keep up with the material at hand. They may report that they are stressed out by the workload or the constant rushing from class to class to activity.

Others still report that they are stressed out by social issues in general. Especially with the current state of the news and media, between violence, school shootings, news about immigrants, or even with the news about illness, disease, or economic pressures, it is easy to recognize that teens, who know that in a short while, they will no longer be entirely under their parents' protective wings, may feel more stressed out than ever.

Peers can also contribute greatly to the stress of teens. Usually, teens find that they are entirely stressed out by their desires to fit in. They fight as hard as they can to be liked, and for good reason—they want to be able to feel like they fit in because every person wants to. In particular, those pressures mount even higher than ever during adolescence, and this can lead to all sorts of peer pressure, which can only lead to more problems in the future.

They tend to be much more irritable or respond with anger more often. This can present as running away to hide in their room, or it can present as teens that suddenly argue and talk back far more than ever.

Teens will also typically show changes in behaviors, oftentimes in their behavioral patterns. If you notice that your teen's schedule and routine have changed dramatically without warning, there is a good chance that they are currently trying to cope better with some stress in their lives.

Sleep changes also become prevalent in teens that are stressed. Keep in mind that teens naturally gravitate toward a schedule in which they sleep later—however, many teens, when stressed out, complain that they cannot fall asleep at all, or, they report constantly feeling tired, even though they got more sleep than ever before.

Children begin to tell themselves that they are bad at what they are trying to do. They may tell themselves that they are ugly or that they are worthless. If you hear your own teen beginning to speak so negatively about themselves that you are concerned, there is a chance that they are suffering through the stress.

Adult Stress

For the average adult, according to the American Psychological Association, roughly 32% report that they experience or suffer from extreme stress, with nearly 20% stating that they are at high levels of their stress at least 15 days, but oftentimes more than that, per month.

This means that the every one in five adults living in America is living under extreme stress and suffering from it at least half of the time. This means that they are going to struggle more often.

The average adult also states that, during the last several years of their lives, stress has gotten worse, and if you think about it, this makes sense. As you get older, you get more responsibilities. You may have a child, and then a few years later have another child or two.

Unfortunately, as your stress ramps up, you are much more likely to suffer from both physical and emotional issues. You may find that you hurt more. You may find that you struggle to digest food, or you may find that your sex drive declines, which can then ripple out and impact your relationship as well.

You can find that you have emotional responses to your stress as well. You may be more irritable than ever, or you may feel nervous or angry. You may constantly feel like you are about to cry.

Stress is something that you cannot control. We have reiterated this repeatedly and for good reason; stress is almost always caused by an external factor that you cannot influence. However, you can work hard to allow yourself to defeat it, little by little. You can work hard to ensure that, at the end of the day, you respond to the stress in the best possible way to make sure that you can cope with it. All you have to do is commit to certain lifestyle changes.

As you read throughout this book, you will be given many different methods that you can use to conquer your own stress. You will learn how you can understand and relieve stress. You will discover how you can control your responses to the stress through firstly learning to identify your triggers. Once you know what causes your stress, you can begin to eliminate the stress as well and that matters greatly. Once you can identify the stress, you can then move on to other aspects of how it is impacting you. You can take a look at the ways in which it can directly influence how you respond as well. It can be that you find out how you can relinquish that stress with recognizing that you must accept what you cannot change.

It involves learning to focus on positive thinking instead of dwelling on the negative or instead of dwelling on things that you cannot control. When you manage to do that, you can begin to master stress. You can reduce the effects that stress has on you because you can begin to let it go. You can become mindful—a state in which you are able to simply exist within the state that you are in.

This may sound convoluted at first, but at its simplest, it is a state of simply focusing on being in that particular moment, of riding the waves within you, no matter whether they are stressed and strong, or they are mild and something that you can really begin to mitigate with relative ease.

No matter what happens, at the end of the day, you do not have to let stress continue to rule your life. You do not have to simply accept that adults, teens, and children will always be stressed. Rather, you can learn to step back from that cycle in which you cannot control it all and you can ensure that you are better able to cope.

Chapter 8: Seeking Stress: How We Self-Sabotage

D espite the fact that people do not want to be stressed, and despite the fact that we all say that we would rather avoid being stressed, we can sometimes fall into self-sabotage. This is rarely intentional—people typically do not want to act in ways that are going to be detrimental to them. People will almost always prefer to behave in ways that are going to be beneficial to them, but when stress has been weighing on them for a while, it gets to a point where they begin to self-sabotage.

Now, consider for a moment that you have a great fear of being too clingy in your relationships. You are constantly worried about bothering your partner. You constantly apologize for what you do and you constantly ask your partner whether or not you are bothering them. You are constantly checking in with them, not because you want to make sure that you are not bothering them, but rather because you want to make sure that you do not feel guilty.

You are trying to assuage your own feelings of doubt. Over time, however, your partner voices that they do not want you to keep apologizing for things that really, in the grand scheme of things, do not matter, and that you should really become more confident and in control of yourself. They tell you that you should be more willing to see yourself as being worthy of the love that they are giving you, and yet you continue to doubt yourself. You continue to ask them whether or not you are bothering them, but eventually, you do annoy them enough that they no longer want to be constantly feeding your fear. They stop bothering with trying to assure you and the relationship may fail entirely.

Let's consider one more example: You know that you are the kind of person that will drink when you get stressed. You know that it is unhealthy and you know that you should not be using alcohol as a method to cope with your stress, and yet you do regularly.

This is not normal, nor is it something that you should be doing. However, instead of taking the very obvious step of making sure that you do not keep alcohol stocked in your home, you continue to buy it after you drink it because you do not want to be out when you want it.

You tell yourself that you will buy it because you will have the self-control to prevent yourself from drinking it when it really matters—even though you do not at all.

This leads to you, the next time that you get stressed, drinking more because it is readily available, allowing you to self-sabotage.

You know that you tend to behave in those ways, and despite knowing that you do not want to drink when you are stressed, you still set yourself up for failure.

All of these are different methods through which self-sabotage can present. They are different ways in which you are doing something that is going to, in some way shape or form, prevent you from succeeding at achieving your goal. They all hurt you in some way, and yet you cannot help yourself. You simply continue to behave in these ways despite the fact that they hurt you and despite the fact that there are many, many different ways that you could behave that would be far healthier for you.

What is Self-Sabotage?

Self-sabotage is a bit of an anomaly as far as behaviors are concerned. While we are designed to focus on how we behave and how we can better ourselves, sometimes, we can get caught up into this cycle in which we damage our self-esteem so much that we are stuck in this negative loop of thinking.

When you sabotage yourself, you are doing something, either intentionally or inadvertently, that will directly inhibit your ability to succeed at whatever it was that you wanted to do. You will essentially be messing yourself up in some way so that you fail at doing what you set out to do, and because you failed to succeed, you then use that failure as justification for why you could never have done it in the future.

Keep in mind that abuse is different from safe use—having a glass of wine with dinner on a regular basis is hardly abuse, especially if you can forego that drink without any real repercussion. If you do not mind having to skip that glass of wine sometimes, then you are probably not self-medicating with it and you simply enjoy it, and the potential benefits that wine can give you.

However, if you have to drink half a bottle of wine every night before bed or you cannot sleep, or if you drink every time that you have something stressful happening the next day, it may be a form of self-sabotage.

Other common self-sabotaging behaviors may be a bit less pronounced to the untrained eye—methods such as comfort eating can also be considered self-sabotage, especially if you are trying to lose weight actively at that point in time.

Some people may procrastinate to self-sabotage—they know that they need to do something and yet they cannot kick themselves into gear quickly enough to get themselves moving toward it. Some people may even resort to hurting themselves or self-mutilating to self-sabotage.

Unfortunately, most people are unaware of what they are doing. They are not trying to sabotage themselves and oftentimes, they do not even realize the connection between their behaviors and the end results. However, they continue to behave in those manners and they continue to struggle. However, self-sabotage is not a life sentence. You can learn to overcome and defeat it if you are able to recognize it, its source, and why it is happening.

Negative Thinking and Negative Automatic Thoughts

Oftentimes, that self-sabotage comes from the fact that people are usually caught up in their own negative thinking patterns. Typically they have what is known as a negative automatic thought underlying everything that is causing them to behave in a certain way.

Most of the time, we all have underlying thoughts as well. These are thoughts that occur so often that we stop noticing them in the first place. Consider for a moment the thought that you are a failure. Perhaps you believe that you are a major failure and that you cannot do anything right. That is a common fear for people that have low self-esteem—they cannot help it. They simply feel like they are a failure for one reason or another.

Those thoughts eventually become a habit, and like all other habits, they happen more or less automatically without really worrying about them. As they happen, the individual that is then going to have those thought floating around in his or her mind without meaning to. They may begin to think those thoughts automatically; they become that voice in the back of their mind, whispering to them just underneath their own conscious perceptions that they are useless and that they cannot do anything right at all. Those thoughts then get ingrained into the cycle.

They go into the interview feeling all of that self-doubt and that self-doubt then stops them from being able to interview properly in the first place. They are so caught up in that feeling of self-doubt and that feeling that they are worthless and that they will make a mistake anyway that they never stop to really consider the way that their actions are impacting them and everyone around them.

They go in without the confidence that they need and the interviewer decides to skip them over. After all, if they lack the confidence and the comfort to be able to interview well, why would they possibly be a good fit for the job? Of course, getting passed up for the interview only further reaffirms that voice in the back of their mind.

They continue to believe that they are incapable of succeeding, and in fact, they may even be more likely to continue to fail simply because they do believe that it is an inherent trait with them rather than anything else. They continue to lack confidence when they go in to interviews and they continue to get turned down for their jobs, over and over and over again. This can really weigh on a person—it can lead to someone simply choosing to give up entirely rather than continuing to try. When it comes right down to it, negative thinking is at the root of all self-sabotage and that negative thinking is also at the root of everything else that goes wrong as well.

The negative thinking can really just exacerbate the stress, making it worse than ever. That negative thinking can lead to the development of all sorts of negative habits and tendencies. That negative thinking can lead to self-sabotage and even self-harm.

Let's take a moment to go over these negative thinking traps that you can fall into, as they can all become incredibly problematic for you. They can all present with very different forms.

Black and white thinking is the kind of thinking that says that things will either be x or y with nothing in between. For example, you may insist that something is boiling hot or freezing cold with nothing in between. However, that is not true at all—there are many temperatures between them that also exist, and likewise, black and white thinking is flawed.

Mind reading is the attempt to assume that you know exactly what someone else is thinking. You may tell yourself that you know exactly what they are thinking, even though in reality, you do not know at all.

This could be, for example, the way that the individual in a previous example said that they were constantly bothering their partner. They assumed to know what their partner was thinking— and that was that they were a bother.

Fortune telling is a sort of way of trying to predict what is going to happen next. This is usually used to try to discourage yourself from trying to do something.

For example, you may find that you tell yourself that you will not succeed anyway, so there is no real purpose or benefit to even trying because it will be a failed attempt no matter what it is that you try to do.

Overgeneralizing is a form in which you assume that just because something happened once that it will happen again. You are essentially trying to simplify things down to make them much worse than they actually have to be. For example, you may tell yourself that you are not going to succeed because you failed before.

Ignoring the positive happens when you sort of wave away any positive aspects that you have. For example, imagine that you are a decent listener—you can sit down and listen to someone else's problems and they tell you that you are a good friend because you are willing to sit and listen.

However, you then wave that away, insisting that anyone can do that and therefore it is not special at all.

Catastrophizing occurs when you begin to think that the worst-case scenarios, which are probably incredibly unlikely, are going to happen. You may realize that your husband has not texted you back in the last 20 minutes so you jump to the conclusion that he must be dead in a ditch somewhere.

Labeling is a form of negative thought that exists just to call someone a name. Essentially, it is assigning a label to someone or something, which is really just an overextension of the overgeneralization problem. When you label someone, or yourself, you are going to basically word something in a way that it will call you a name. For example, you may say that you are a failure after you have failed. You assign the name to yourself rather than recognizing that you are not actually a failure at all, and rather, you have failed once.

Self-blame refers to trying to essentially personalize everything. You are repeatedly assuming that you are the problem whenever you see someone having any sort of problem and you assume that it will be on you to figure out how to fix it. For example, you may see that your partner is angry that day and think that it must have been your own fault.

All of these forms of negative thinking can directly relate back to your own attempt to self-sabotage. Usually, one of these will be the underlying thought pattern that is egging you and your behaviors on. You will be thinking in these negative ways and those thoughts will create the self-sabotaging behaviors that you are trying to defeat.

Remember, just because you know that these thoughts are there does not mean that you have to continue to live by them. You can begin to defeat them. You can learn how you can overcome those negative thinking patterns and we will be looking at this closely in the future chapters as well.

Chapter 9: Results of Stress: Mood Disorders and Disordered Thinking

S tress really wears on the body. It can cause higher blood pressure and heart rates. It can cause diabetes. It can cause cardiovascular disease. It is able to do all of this because it is so destructive. It is able to do this because it is able to disrupt the body in many different ways that can be incredibly damaging. It can disrupt the body through the way that it influences the hormones in the body.

If you are under enough stress for long enough, one of the most common results is beginning to suffer from mental health disorders that impact the mood. These are very common in people that are under stress, and for good reason.

However, when there is something that your body deems to be threatening, you suddenly enter a sympathetic response instead. This is essentially the vagus nerve stopping—when the vagus nerve is active, it is able to sort of balance out the sympathetic nervous system, which is responsible for the fight or flight response. As soon as the vagus nerve stops, it essentially releases the reins and lets t hat sympathetic nervous system take control.

When that happens, you begin to feel anxious. Your body shifts from a state of relaxation to a state of stress. It is ready to either fight or it is ready to run away—whichever is going to be the most likely to let you survive.

When you are under chronic stress, you are able to feel this activation. You recognize that, at the end of the day, you are stuck in that constant state of anxiety. That can begin to weigh on you, little by little, until it overwhelms you completely.

When that happens, you wind up suffering more. You are stuck in this state of anxiety in which you are always afraid that someone or something is threatening you. Your body never get to relax, and that can really wreak havoc on your emotional state.

Chronic stress oftentimes becomes disordered thinking. The more that you stress out about what is going on, the more you begin to feel like you are overwhelmed by it.

The more overwhelmed you become, the more likely it is that you will continue to suffer. The more that you suffer, the more likely that it is that you will begin to see real consequences to what is going on around you.

They are many different conditions that can lead to problems for people, and stress can typically exacerbate them. When you live under stress, you find that, at the end of the day, it will exacerbate the moods that you are feeling.

Mood disorders are surprisingly common—those who have some mental health issue typically feel marginalized or isolated, but the reality is that roughly 20% of the population in the US alone reports feeling depressive symptoms within a month. 12% of people report that they feel depressed at least twice a year.

This means that, in a group of people, there is a very good chance that at least one, if not more, suffer from some degree of depression, anxiety, or from other mood disorders as well.

These disorders can be incredibly disruptive and even embarrassing for those that suffer from them. People do not want to admit when they do suffer from these disorders, but at the end of the day, they are nothing to e ashamed of.

Treatment is available for these mood disorders that you may suffer from as well. They exist in many different capacities—some people get depressed. Some suffer from bipolar depression. Some suffer from many of the varying forms of anxiety, which on its own is not a mood disorder, but it does occur as a result of the negative effects of stress that occur.

Stress and Your Mental Health

Now, we know one thing for certain—when you suffer from stress, it has a major impact on the mental health of the individual. This is for a very good reason—when you suffer under the effects of stress, it literally changes the way that your brain looks. It changes the effectiveness of your brain and the way that this is done is through the ratio of grey and white matter found within the brain.

When you look at the brain, you can usually identify two types of matter: white matter and grey matter. The white matter is responsible for producing connections within the brain, allowing for the brain to send messages further and quicker, allowing for essential functions to happen rapidly. Grey matter is responsible for the abilities to think, learn, pay attention, and remember things.

Those who are chronically stressed show higher levels of white matter as opposed to the grey matter that is responsible for that higher level cognition that is commonly associated with growing up.

The brain is a wonderful, pliable organ and it is very good at rolling with whatever situations that you put it into. Just as it was able to be rewired by stress, you can also rewire it in other ways as well. We will be looking at doing that shortly.

Anxiety and Stress

Anxiety is oftentimes related closely to stress.

When you are stressed, it is a normal reaction to feel anxiety—that is your way of sort of dealing with it. Anxiety and stress, for many people, are entirely synonymous. However, anxiety itself is a very specific feeling. Anxiety is that feeling that you are worried about the stress that you are under. It is that feeling of fear—that dread within your chest that you feel deeply and that you are certain will overwhelm you.

When you suffer from anxiety, you oftentimes find that it can become exacerbated during times of stress. It becomes that emotional reaction to your stress that you are enduring.

The good news is, anxiety is something that you can begin to control. You cannot control your stressors—but you can control the response, and that is what we are considering within this chapter.

Typically, people feel restless when they are anxious—they are right on the verge of that flight response.

They are usually easily drained thanks to the expense of energy while they are in this sort of emotional activation. They may also suffer from panic attacks in which they feel like they are out of control or even like they may be about to die.

Anxiety is no joke, and usually, stress is considered one of the main factors that can contribute to it. When you are stressed, you are naturally going to be more inclined to feel anxious. You are more likely to feel like you cannot control what is going on simply because of the way that it will make you respond to the world around you.

When you are stressed out like this, you oftentimes find that you struggle greatly with your anxiety symptoms, and almost ironically, the more anxious you become, the more likely you are to also struggle with your stress.

Depression and Stress

Stress, when it becomes chronic, can also lead to depression in those that are already susceptible to it as well. Stress, whether positive or negative, can be overwhelming.

It can be something that becomes too much for the individual— they cannot properly cope with the changes that they have to make and because they get stuck in those feelings, they begin to shut down.

Depression is essentially a shutdown of the mind. In part, the depression that you may suffer from is a direct response to the stress of the body that has been under chronic stress for far too long. In particular, stress increases stress hormones.

Stress hormones, such as cortisol, can then begin to weigh heavily on the brain. They can essentially drain the brain of its ability to properly function through cutting the rate at which the brain produces serotonin.

Serotonin is an essential neurotransmitter that is there to help you—it is there to regulate your normal biological processes, such as sleep, eating, waking, libido, and positive moods. However, when you do not have enough serotonin in your brain, you find that there is very little way for you to properly function.

You find that you feel sluggish. You feel like you cannot get up. When your body has been under stress for long enough without being able to regulate itself out, depression then may occur as a response. The depression is your body's way of figuring out how it can shut off the stress.

Anger and Stress

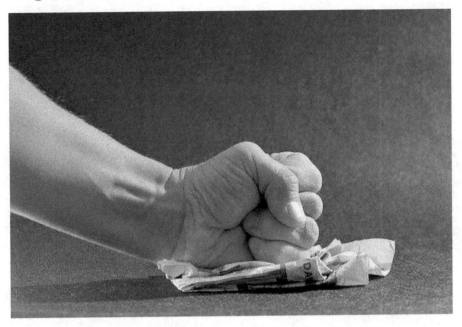

Like anxiety, anger is another common response to stress. Anger is like the other side of the coin to anxiety. While anxiety comes with its desire to escape from the stress in some way, anger comes with the desire to fight it off.

Anger, it is important to note, is almost always secondary—the anger that you feel is typically in direct response to your body trying to come up with some way, shape, or form that it can defeat the anxiety or fear.

When you are under too much stress, you may notice that you become much more irritable than ever before. You may find that you are difficult to calm down and difficult to persuade to relax. You may be more willing to lash out at loved ones than you should be. You may deal with the anger poorly, but you do not have to— not really, anyway. When it comes down to it, anger is something that can be controlled. Like depression and anxiety, anger is a response to the stress that you feel, and as a response, it is within the realm of your control, should you choose to do so. You can stop yourself from becoming so irrationally angry in the first place. You can learn to recognize when you are angry so you can then slow down your response. You can work in many ways to sort of mitigate out the anger that you are feeling. You can work hard to find a way that you can calm it down and therefore allow yourself to better respond.

Conclusion

Remember the information that has been provided to you. Do not forget the fact that the secret to a good day is to have a good night and do not forget just how heavily that a lack of sleep that is healthy and restful can put on your mind. Do not forget that you are the only one that is responsible for the sleep that you need, and that you can help to promote and facilitate it with ease.

From here, all that is left to do is to change your habits for the better. If you want the fullest effects of everything, from the exercises that you are going through to the sleep that you are getting to the way that you are thinking, you must ensure that you embrace everything that this book has offered you.

This means that you *need* to keep up with it. You need to remember that these changes that were encouraged to you are lifestyle changes. They are ways of life.

They are not simply there to be used for a week and magically, for life, fix your sleep problems; rather, they must be used regularly to continue to see the benefit.

CPSIA information can be obtained
at www.ICGtesting.com
Printed in the USA
BVHW040346190521
607637BV00005BA/878

9 781802 251050